ISSN 2475-2061

Dediu Newsletter

Author: Michael M. Dediu

I0192449

Monthly news, reviews, comments and suggestions for a better and wiser world

Vol. 3, Nr. 6 (30), 6 May 2019

DERC Publishing House

Tewksbury (Boston), Massachusetts, U. S. A.
For subscriptions please use the contact form at www.derc.com

Published and printed in the
United States of America
On the Great Seal of the United States are included:
E Pluribus Unum (Out of many, one)
Annuit Coeptis (He has approved of the undertakings)
Novus Ordo Seclorum (New order of the ages)

Dediu, Michael M.

Dediu Newsletter Vol 3, Number 5 (29), 6 April 2019
Monthly reviews, comments and suggestions for a better and wiser world

ISSN 2475-2061
ISBN 978-1-939757-90-6

Preface

April 2019 started with World Health Day on 7th, and there are many good medical news, as well as other good news: a new wearable sensor monitors health through sweat, using nanotech; using AI, IBM helped NASA fix one of its satellites, which is on a geosynchronous equatorial orbit; Comcast and T-Mobile launched anti-robocalling feature; Amazon has new investments in air cargo transport companies; researchers found that nanomaterial helps heal damage after a heart attack.

In this 6[h] newsletter of the third volume, the 30th in total, we included the most relevant news, in a balanced approach, usually directly from the source, to help the general public better understand the realities around us. We included also several nice photos - I thank my wife for her photo assistance. Being well and correctly informed is a sine qua non requirement for everybody, in order to make the right decisions for the future.

Enjoy this newsletter and be optimist!

Michael M. Dediu, Ph. D.

Tewksbury (Boston), U. S. A., 6 May 2019

USA, Bretton Woods: The Gold Room in the Mount Washington Resort (1902, elevation 500 m, by Joseph Stickney (1840 – 1903, coal business)), where the documents of the United Nations Monetary and Financial Conference (1 – 22 July 1944, 730 delegates from 44 Allied nations, at Bretton Woods (12 km west of Mount Washington (1917 m), 250 km north of Boston), established the International Monetary Fund and the World Bank. The Bretton Woods system worked for 27 years, until 1971) were signed. On the right - a table with the flags of the 44 Allied nations.

Table of Contents

Table of Contents

Italy, Milano: 30 Sep 2008, in Piazza del Duomo, looking southeast to the north side of il Duomo (Basilica Cattedrale metropolitana di Santa Maria Nascente, 1386-1965 (579 years), capacity 40,000, length 158.5 m, width 92 m, maximum height 108 m, 135 spires, materials: brick and Candoglia marble, architects: Donato Bramante (1444-1514), Leonardo da Vinci (1452-1519), Giulio Romano (1499-1546), Pellegrino Tibaldi (1527-1596)). On May 20, 1805, Napoleon Bonaparte (1769-1821), about to be crowned King of Italy, ordered the façade to be finished by Pellicani. For this, a statue of Napoleon was placed at the top of one of the spires. Napoleon was crowned King of Italy at the Duomo on May 26, 1805.

United States of America

(Population 324.4 M, rank 3, growth 0.7%. Free: 89 of 100. Area 9.52 M km^2, rank 4.).

Reports: The government is now a money-printing, check-writing, and wealth-redistribution machine that costs trillions.

Reports: America's biggest economic challenge is its demographic decline.

Reports: The deficit has ballooned in recent months. CBO breaks down the source of the deficit, dividing between reductions in revenue and increases in spending — and the comparison isn't even close. It's spending-driven all the way. Spending is and will remain the root of the problem, and deficits will rise until policymakers summon the courage to get spending under control.

Reports: Don Parrish, the American Farm Bureau Federation's senior director of regulatory relations, like many others, explained again why the "Waters of the United States" (WOTUS) rule, passed by the previous administration, hurts everybody, and especially farmers and those living close to small man-made ditches, and therefore should be eliminated.

Reports: U.S. budget deficit is running 15% higher than a year ago.

Reports: This year, the government in Washington will spend a staggering $35,148 per household and collect $26,677 per household in taxes. The resulting budget deficit of $8,471 per household will bring the total national debt to $177,000 per household. Federal spending has soared nearly $7,000 per household since 2007.

Reports: There is in America a kind of media overindulgence, which is somehow not helping the country, exploiting partisan divisions, and absorbing so much time and energy that it slows America in trying to analyze the real dangers that could destroy the country. Mueller reported on 448 pages, after a nearly two-year effort, which involved 19 lawyers, 40 staff, more than 2,800 subpoenas, nearly 500 search warrants, around 500 witnesses, and spent more than $25 M. The report found no laws broken; however, the news media does not want to give up just because two years of work by 14 highly motivated Democrat lawyers did not come with serious charges. It is well known that there is 92% negative news coverage of the administration.

There are now college classes on how not to be fooled by the news. Journalism is at risk not just from government, but from media types who see their jobs as protecting some politicians from embarrassment.

Higher-education appropriations now exceed those before the recession in only six states: Alaska, California, Hawaii, New York, Wisconsin, and Wyoming."

People celebrate the boom in private education.

Reports: The true root of America's fiscal insanity is entitlement spending. Nondefense discretionary spending is projected to represent about 15% of federal spending in 2019, or about $669 B out of the expected budget of over $4.4 T. Congress could eliminate all nondefense discretionary spending, and still run a large budget deficit of more than $300 B. This is because mandatory spending, including entitlement programs like Medicare and Social Security, and interest on publicly held debt, will increase above historical averages.

Reports: The Food and Drug Administration (FDA) has rule-making practices that made 98% of its regulations, since 2001, unconstitutional. That's the figure which was uncovered in a comprehensive study examining 2,952 Health and Human Services (HHS) regulations issued during a 17-year period. If a federal agency enforces even one invalid rule against Americans, it breaches the public trust, and the rule of law. Enforcing 100 invalid rules would constitute an unprecedented threat to democratic principles from a lawless agency. What was found at FDA is that from early 2001 to early 2018, FDA issued 1,860 unconstitutional rules.

Reports: Very abusive people send many robocalls. These abusive robodialers are busier than ever, because the authorities don't stop them. Likely related to Voice over Internet Protocol (VOIP) technology, mass calling, and the ability to display fake caller ID information, are both quick and inexpensive, making the calls easy for criminals. According to the Federal Communications Commission (FCC), nearly 2.4 billions of robocalls are made every month, which means over 900 abusive robocalls per second. These abuses must be stopped by authorities.

Puerto Rico: (Population 3.6 M, rank 134, decrease 0.1%; an unincorporated territory of the United States, located in the northeast Caribbean Sea, 1,600 km southeast of Miami, Florida.).

United Nations. There are 195 officially recognized countries. Around 44,000 people work for the United Nations. There is a wide range of jobs: Researchers, IT-specialists, lawyers, experts on finance and administration, or translators work at the New York headquarters, at the official locations, or at specialized agencies. More than half of the UN's workforce is employed in the field, in projects of humanitarian aid, or on peace missions.

USA, Massachusetts, Cape Cod: The Pilgrims Monument in the center of Provincetown, built with granite between 1907 and 1910, commemorates the first landfall of the Pilgrims in 1620, and the signing in Provincetown Harbor of the Mayflower Compact.

China, Japan, and neighbors

China: (Population 1.4 B, rank 1, growth 0.4%. Freedom House reports for 2019: Not Free (15 of 100). Area 9.59 M km^2, rank 3).

3 April 2019, Xinhua: President Xi Jinping, also general secretary of the Communist Party of China (CPC) Central Committee and chairman of the Central Military Commission, delivers a speech at the central conference on political and legal work in Beijing, capital of China. The conference was held in Beijing on Jan 15 and 16, 2019. Chinese President Xi Jinping has urged civil affairs authorities to better fulfill their duties, by focusing on poverty alleviation, special groups and public concerns.

Xi made the statement in an instruction read at a national civil affairs conference held in Beijing Tuesday, 2 April.

Identifying civil affairs work as a fundamental aspect of social development, Xi called on Party committees and governments at various levels to be committed to a people-centered approach, strengthen leadership over the civil affairs work, and enhance civil affairs services at the primary level. Civil affairs organs should better perform their duties of ensuring basic livelihood security, strengthening social governance at the primary level, and providing basic social services, to make new contributions to finishing the building of a moderately prosperous society in all respects, and turning China into a modern socialist country, Xi said.

When meeting with participants of the meeting, Premier Li Keqiang acknowledged the progress made in this area and stressed the tough tasks ahead. Li asked the civil affairs departments to implement the policies of the CPC Central Committee and State Council, and make sure people living below the minimum living standards, and those in exceptional difficulties, receive sufficient support.

Reports: For China, war with the United States never ended — and likely never will. Some business journalists are supported by China to write favorably about China's leaders, government, official state news agency Xinhua, and their activities.

Reports: Silence plus Conformity = Complicity — this is the university life in China today. New deputy director of Beijing's liaison office makes first public remarks: Calls on Hongkongers to be patriotic, study Chinese history, and help develop nation. The punishment of a prominent scholar means no intellectual freedom in China.

History: The Terracotta Warriors are terracotta sculptures depicting the armies of Qin Shi Huang, the first Emperor of China. It is a form of funerary art buried with the emperor in 210–209 BC.

History: In Dazu County, 165 km west from Chongqing, and 1,500 km southwest of Beijing, there are more than 40 sites of stone carvings with over 50,000 statues of Buddha completed from the later Tang Dynasty (618 – 907) to the Song Dynasty (960 – 1279).

Reports: China releases new syllabus for military courses in universities.

23 April 2019. Xinhua: Chinese President and Central Military Commission Chairman Xi Jinping holds a group meeting with the heads of foreign delegations invited to the multinational naval events marking the 70th anniversary of the founding of the Chinese People's Liberation Army Navy in Qingdao, east China's Shandong province, on April 23, 2019.

Chinese President Xi Jinping on Tuesday, 23 April, called for concerted efforts to safeguard maritime peace and build a maritime community with a shared future. Xi, also chairman of the Central Military Commission, made the remarks during a group meeting with the heads of foreign delegations invited to participate in the multinational naval events marking the 70th founding anniversary of the Chinese People's Liberation Army (PLA) Navy.

Oceans are of great significance to the survival and development of humanity, as they breed life, connect the world, and promote development, Xi said. "The blue planet humans inhabit is not divided into islands by the oceans, but is connected by the oceans to form a community with a shared future, where people of all countries share weal and woe," he said. Xi said maritime peace and tranquility concern the security and interests of all countries, and need to be jointly maintained and cherished.

Join hands for maritime peace

"The peace-loving Chinese people long for peace, and will unswervingly stay on the path of peaceful development," Xi said.

China pursues a national defense policy that is defensive in nature, and champions new thinking on common, comprehensive, cooperative, and sustainable security, he noted. "Holding high the banner of win-win cooperation, the Chinese military is committed to creating a security environment featuring equality, mutual trust, fairness and justice, joint participation and shared benefits," he said. As the mainstay of forces at sea, the navies shoulder heavy responsibilities for safeguarding maritime peace and order, Xi said. Nations should enhance mutual respect, equal treatment and mutual trust, strengthen maritime dialogue and exchanges, deepen practical naval cooperation, and pursue a mutually beneficial and win-win approach to maritime security, he said.

Xi called for joint efforts to address common threats and challenges at sea, and safeguard maritime peace and tranquility.

At present, ocean-based cooperation in market, technology, information, culture, and other areas is steadily deepening, Xi said. The reason for China to propose jointly building the 21st Century Maritime Silk Road, Xi said, is to facilitate maritime connectivity, pragmatic cooperation in various fields, and the development of the "blue economy," as well as to promote the integration of maritime cultures and to improve maritime wellbeing. "The Chinese armed forces are willing to work with their foreign counterparts to actively contribute to maritime development and prosperity," Xi said.

"We should cherish oceans as we treat our lives," Xi said. He noted that China has fully participated in the formulation and implementation of maritime governance mechanism and related rules within the UN framework, and implemented the goal of sustainable marine development. China pays great attention to the building of marine ecological civilization, persistently intensifies the prevention and treatment of marine pollution, protects marine biodiversity, and orderly exploits the marine resources, in order to leave a blue sky and clean ocean for future generations, he said.

Xi also said that the Chinese PLA Navy will continue to strengthen exchanges and cooperation with foreign navies, actively shoulder its international responsibilities, safeguard the security of international waterways, and provide more public goods for maritime security.

Maritime community with shared future

"The sea is vast for it embraces so many rivers," Xi cited, calling for more and better consultations when there is an issue, instead of resorting to violence or threatening with violence.

All countries should consult as equals, improve the mechanism for communication in face of crises, strengthen regional security cooperation, and promote the proper solution to maritime disputes, according to Xi. A high-level seminar on building a maritime community with a shared future will be held as part of the multinational naval events, he said.

Xi expressed hope that the delegations would gather their ideas, build consensus and contribute their wisdom to building a maritime community with a shared future.

Commander-in-Chief of the Royal Thai Navy Admiral Luechai Ruddit, on behalf of the heads of foreign delegations, thanked Xi for the meeting, and congratulated the PLA Navy on its 70th founding anniversary.

He also thanked the Chinese government, military and navy for their contributions to and efforts in advancing a community with a shared future for humanity, including a maritime community with a shared future. He expressed belief that the concept and proposal of a maritime community with a shared future will promote cooperation among navies and contribute to maritime peace and prosperity.

Xi took a group photo with the heads of foreign delegations before the meeting. Xu Qiliang, Ding Xuexiang, Wei Fenghe and Wang Yi were present at the meeting.

25 April 2019. Vladimir Putin arrived in Beijing for a working visit, where he will attend the second Belt and Road International Forum.

History: Xinhua: Proposed by Chinese President Xi Jinping in 2013, the Belt and Road Initiative comprises the Silk Road Economic Belt and the 21st Century Maritime Silk Road, and aims to build trade and infrastructure networks connecting Asia with Europe and Africa along and beyond the ancient Silk Road routes.

26 April 2019. Vladimir Putin attended the second Belt and Road Forum for International Cooperation, in Beijing. Vladimir Putin spoke at the opening ceremony of the forum business program. The Belt and Road Forum takes place in Beijing, on April 25–27.

26 April 2019. Beijing is hosting talks between Vladimir Putin and President of the People's Republic of China, Xi Jinping.

27 April 2019. Vladimir Putin took part in the first roundtable discussion at the Belt and Road Forum for International Cooperation in Beijing.

29 April 2019. Reports: President Xi Jinping raised a glass to his signature foreign policy project at a Belt and Road conference in Beijing on Saturday, 27 April, touting "open, clean and green" infrastructure deals worth more than $64 B. In a separate statement, China said it signed a memorandum of understanding with various countries including Italy, Peru, Barbados, Luxembourg, and Jamaica. Data from Refinitiv show the total value of projects in the New Silk Road at $3.67 T, spanning countries in Asia, Europe, Africa, Oceania, and South America.

Reports: The emerging China hypersonic weapons are a great threat to surface vessels at sea.

1 May 2019. Xinhua: Chinese President Xi Jinping, also general secretary of the Communist Party of China Central Committee and chairman of the Central Military Commission, addressed a gathering marking the centenary of the May Fourth Movement, at the Great Hall of the People in Beijing, capital of China, April 30, 2019. Xi Jinping called on the country's young people to be patriotic and strive for the bright prospect of national rejuvenation.

The May Fourth Movement started with mass student protests on May 4, 1919 against the government's response to the Treaty of Versailles that imposed unfair treaties on China, and undermined the country's sovereignty after the World War I. It then triggered a national campaign to overthrow the old society, and promote new ideas, including science, democracy and Marxism.

Wang Huning presided over the gathering. Other Chinese leaders Li Keqiang, Li Zhanshu, Wang Yang, Zhao Leji, Han Zheng, and Wang Qishan were also present. Xi said the May Fourth Movement was a great patriotic and revolutionary campaign pioneered by advanced young intellectuals, and joined by the people from all walks of life, to resolutely fight imperialism and feudalism.

With its mighty force, the movement inspired the ambition and confidence of the Chinese people and nation to realize national rejuvenation, Xi added.

Patriotism

Xi said the May Fourth Movement gave birth to the great spirit centered on patriotism, progress, democracy and science, with patriotism at the core. "As long as the banner of patriotism is being held high, the Chinese people can unleash great powers in the endeavors to transform China and the world," Xi said.

The essence of patriotism is having unified love for the country, the Party and socialism, Xi added, urging young Chinese to follow the instructions and guidance of the Party, and remain dedicated to the country and the people. Young people are also urged to establish belief in Marxism, faith in socialism with Chinese characteristics, as well as confidence in the Chinese Dream of national rejuvenation.

National rejuvenation

Xi said young people always play a vanguard role in realizing national rejuvenation. In the new era, the theme and direction of Chinese youth movement, and the mission of Chinese young people, Xi said, are to uphold the leadership of the CPC, and work along with the people to realize the two centenary goals, and the Chinese Dream of national rejuvenation. Xi said Chinese youth of the new era should bear their responsibilities of the times, and carry on the spirit of arduous struggle.

He urged them to hone abilities and nurture fine morality.

Xi also encouraged young people to not only care about their family and country, but also have concerns for humanity.

Youth work

Xi said nurturing the young generation is the whole Party's political responsibility. "We should listen to young people's views on social issues and phenomena, as well as their opinions and advices on the work of the Party and the government," Xi said.

"Even if they express harsh or partial criticism, we should correct our mistakes, when we have made any, and guard against them, when we have not," he added.

Xi called on the Party to address young people's concerns, and asked the Communist Youth League of China to unite and lead the young people to strive for the national rejuvenation.

"Young friends," Xi said near the end of his speech. "Let your youth shine even more in the sacrifice for the country, the people, the Chinese nation, and humanity."

Hong Kong. (Population 7.3 M, rank 104, growth 0.8%. Partly Free: 61 of 100).

10 April 2019. Reports: Hong Kong's stock market capitalization overnight surpassed Japan's for the first time since the Chinese equity bubble popped in 2015. It makes the territory's equity market the world's third largest in value at $5.78 T, behind only the U.S. and mainland China. Boosted by internet giant Tencent Holdings, the Hang Seng Index has climbed 17% so far this year vs. the 8.2% advance of Japan's Topix Index.

Macau (Population 622 K, rank 167, growth 1.7 %.)

Reports: Macau's April casino revenue posts worst drop in nearly three years.

Taiwan: (Population 23.6 M, rank 56, growth 0.3%. Free, 91 of 100).

18 April 2019. Xinhua: The U.S. arms sale plan unveiled Monday,15 April, is a dangerous move that will only aggravate the already complex and grim situation across the Taiwan Strait.

The U.S. government has approved a possible 500 M-U.S. dollars military sale to Taiwan, claiming that the move will help to improve the security and defensive capability of the recipient.

Subsequently, Taiwan leader Tsai Ing-wen expressed "gratitude," saying that the arms sale was "timely." The situation across the Taiwan Strait, which is already complicated and grim, is worsening as the United States has been using Taiwan to contain China, while the Taiwan administration kept seeking foreign intervention.

The Taiwan question concerns China's sovereignty and territorial integrity, and is the most important and sensitive issue in China-U.S. relations.

The U.S. arms sales to Taiwan constitutes a serious violation of international law, the basic norms governing international relations, the one-China principle, and the three Sino-U.S. joint communiques, and undermine China's sovereignty and security interests.

China's firm opposition to such arms sales is consistent and firm.

Since the current U.S. administration took office, it has constantly played the "Taiwan card" to contain China, especially in arms sales to Taiwan, and military exchanges between the United States and

Taiwan. This has seriously damaged China-U.S. relations, and jeopardized peace and stability across the Taiwan Strait.

The Taiwan question, which concerns China's core interests and the national bond of the Chinese people, brooks no external interference. The U.S. administration has once again stirred up sensitive nerves in the Taiwan Strait. Its gross interference in China's internal affairs has aroused the strong indignation of the Chinese people on both sides of the Strait.

Some Taiwan organizations and people protested outside the American Institute in Taiwan (AIT) in Taipei, condemning U.S. arms sales to Taiwan and demanding "no war, only peace," and "Taiwan is not a pawn for the United States." Therefore, we would like to advise the U.S. side to clearly recognize the high sensitivity and serious harm of arms sales to Taiwan, correct mistakes, honor its commitments, and handle Taiwan-related issues in a prudent and proper manner, in accordance with the one-China principle, and the provisions of the three Sino-U.S. joint communiques. Taiwan's current Democratic Progressive Party (DPP) administration, which is teetering on the brink of collapse, was overjoyed at the U.S. arms sales as if it had been given a "straw to save its life."

Tsai Ing-wen and the DPP administration have escalated provocations against the Chinese mainland, created disturbances recently and cooperated with the United States in vigorously clamoring the so-called "military threat" from the mainland.

In the face of next year's general election on the island, Tsai and the DPP will not hesitate to let Taiwan serve as a pawn for forces of external interference, in order to protect their power, regardless of the safety and well-being of the Taiwanese people.

This party has not only misjudged the situation but also deviated from the people's heart. U.S. weapons cannot guarantee Taiwan's security. Tsai and the DPP cannot secure their power and position by seeking foreign interference, or threatening the people.

Tsai, the DPP and "Taiwan independence" separatist elements should not play with fire, or even think about it. They are doomed to be alone in the face of the pressure of their own actions.

On April 17, 1895, 124 years ago, the Treaty of Shimonoseki was signed between Japan and the Qing dynasty, securing foreigner's (Japan) occupation of Taiwan for half a century, until 1945. It left lasting, painful memories for all Chinese. Today's China will never allow the historical tragedy of national division to repeat itself.

No one and no force should underestimate the determination and capability of the Chinese in safeguarding national sovereignty and territorial integrity.

Japan, Tokyo, 27 November 2008, Emperor Gardens

Japan (Population 127.5 M, rank 11, decrease 0.2%. Free, 96 of 100).

9 April 2019. Reports: TOKYO, Japan - Last week, the Japan Aerospace Exploration Agency (JAXA) announced its Hayabusa2 spacecraft had dropped what it dubbed a Small Carry-on Impactor (SCI) onto the asteroid Ryugu, and caused to produce a planned explosion, to create a crater.

30 April 2019. Reports: Three decades after he ascended the Chrysanthemum Throne, Emperor Akihito on Tuesday, 30 April, became Japan's first monarch in more than two centuries to abdicate, passing the symbolic role to his eldest son in a brief, unadorned ceremony at the Imperial Palace.

Akihito, 85, the son of the emperor Hirohito, relinquished the throne to Crown Prince Naruhito, 59, who will receive the sacred imperial regalia in a ceremony on Wednesday, 1st May, morning. The last emperor to abdicate was Kokaku, in 1817.

When Akihito took over the throne in 1989, it was after his father had suffered a prolonged illness. Akihito, who was treated for prostate cancer in 2003, and underwent heart surgery in 2012, may have wished to avoid subjecting his son to a period of such limbo.

But the decision to abdicate was not the emperor's alone to make, and he ultimately had to wait three years after first expressing his desire to step down. The abdication required a special act of Parliament, passed in 2017. The law applies only to him and not to future emperors. With Akihito's abdication, he becomes known as the Heisei emperor, after the name given to the era in which he reigned. Imperial custom dictates that the reign of each emperor is accompanied by a name for his term in power. The new era, known as Reiwa, begins on Wednesday, 1st May.

30 April 2019. Vladimir Putin sent his greetings to Emperor Akihito of Japan.

1 May 2019. Vladimir Putin sent greetings to Emperor Naruhito of Japan.

Afghanistan: (Population 35.5 M, rank 40, growth 2.5%. Not free: 24 of 100).

South Korea: (Population 50.9 M, rank 27, growth 0.4%. Free, 82 of 100).

North Korea: (Population 25.4 M, rank 52, growth 0.5%. Not free: 3 of 100).

11 April 2019. Reports: Kim Jong-un threatens those levying sanctions on North Korea.

12 April 2019. Vladimir Putin congratulated Kim Jong-un on his re-election as Chairman of the State Affairs Commission of the Democratic People's Republic of Korea.

18 April 2019. Reports: There are news of renewed weapons tests by North Korea.

25 April 2019. Russky Island (south of Vladivostok, Russia) hosted talks between the President of Russia and Chairman of the State Affairs Commission of the Democratic People's Republic of Korea, Kim Jong-un. The talks started with a one-on-one

conversation between the two leaders, with members of national delegations joining the consultations later on.

The leader of the Democratic People's Republic of Korea has arrived in Vladivostok at the invitation of the President of Russia. This is the first meeting between Vladimir Putin and Kim Jong-un, as well as the first foreign visit by the Chairman of the State Affairs Commission of the Democratic People's Republic of Korea since his re-election to this post. After the consultations, an official reception was held on behalf of the President of Russia in honor of Chairman of the State Affairs Commission of the Democratic People's Republic of Korea, Kim Jong-un.

Vietnam (Population 95.5 M, rank 15, growth 1%. Not free, 20 of 100).

Laos (Population. 6.8 M, rank 106, growth 1.5%. Not free: 12 of 100).

Cambodia (Population 16 M, rank 71, growth 1.5%. Not Free 31 of 100).

Mongolia (Population 3 M, rank 137, growth 1.6%. Free 85 of 100)

Nepal: (Population 29.3 M, rank 48, growth 1.1%. Partly free 52 of 100).

Russia, Switzerland, Eastern Europe

Russia: (Population 143.9 M, rank 9, growth 0%. Not free: 20 of 100. Area 17 M km^2, rank 1)

Reports: Russia did not have a war with the U.S. – and likely will never have.

9 April 2019. Vladimir Putin attended the plenary session of the 5th International Arctic Forum "The Arctic: Territory of Dialogue". The theme of the session is "The Arctic: An Ocean of Opportunity". President of the Republic of Finland, Sauli Niinistö, President of the Republic of Iceland, Guðni Thorlacius Jóhannesson, Prime Minister of the Kingdom of Norway, Erna Solberg, and Prime Minister of the Kingdom of Sweden, Stefan Löfven, are taking part in the discussion.

Reports: In 2018, the Russian federal budget had a surplus of 2.6% of GDP.

Reports: This year is dedicated to the anniversaries of the great Russian composers Nikolai Rimsky-Korsakov (March 18, 1844, Tikhvin, near Novgorod, Russia — June 21, 1908, Lyubensk, Russia, aged 64.2) – 175 years from his birth, and Modest Mussorgsky (March 21, 1839, Karevo, Russia - March 28, 1881, Saint Petersburg, Russia, aged 42 years and 7 days) – 180 years from his birth.

Switzerland: (Population 8.4 M, rank 99, growth 0.9%. Free: 96 of 100).

Reports: Swiss scientists make synthetic bacterial genome using computers.

Austria: (Population 8.7 M, rank 98, growth 0.3%. Free: 95 of 100).

Poland: (Population 38.1 M, rank 37, decrease 0.1%. Free: 89 of 100).

Croatia: (Population 4.1 M, rank 129, decrease 0.6%. Free: 87 of 100).

Finland: (Population 5.5 M, rank 116, growth 0.4%. Free: 100 of 100).

9 April 2019. Vladimir Putin had a conversation with President of Finland, Sauli Niinistö, on the sidelines of the 5th International Arctic Forum "The Arctic: Territory of Dialogue".

Romania (Population: 19.6 M, rank 59, decrease 0.5%. Free: 84 of 100)

Moldova: (Population: 4 M, rank 132, decrease 0.2%. Partly Free: 62 of 100).

Belarus: (Population: 9.4 M, rank 93, decrease 0.1%. Not Free: 20 of 100).

Bulgaria: (Population: 7 M, rank 105, decrease 0.7%. Free: 80 of 100).

Slovenia: (Population: 2 M, rank 148, growth 0.1%. Free: 92 of 100).

Hungary: (Population: 9.7 M, rank 91, decrease 0.3%. Free: 76 of 100)

Ukraine: (Population: 44.2 M, rank 32, decrease 0.5%. Partly free: 61 of 100).

Latvia: (Population: 1.9 M, rank 150, decrease 1.1%. Free: 87 of 100).

Lithuania: (Population: 2.8 M, rank 141, decrease 0.6%. Free: 91 of 100).

Estonia: (Population: 1.3 M, rank 155, decrease 0.2%. Free: 94 of 100).

18 April 2019. Vladimir Putin met with President of Estonia, Kersti Kaljulaid, who is in Moscow on a working visit.

Serbia: (including Kosovo: Population: 8.7 M, rank 97, decrease 0.3%. Free: 76 of 100). 26 April 2019. Vladimir Putin had a meeting with President of the Republic of Serbia, Aleksandar Vucic, in Beijing, China. The leaders discussed bilateral and regional issues.

Kosovo ((Disputed: recognized by 110 countries, and not recognized by Serbia, Russia, and others) Population: 1.8 M, Partly free: 52 of 100).

Bosnia and Herzegovina: (Population: 3.5 M, rank 135, decrease 0.3%. Partly free: 55 of 100).

Turkey: (Population 80.7 M, rank 19, growth 1.2%. Partly free: 38 of 100).
8 April 2019. Talks between Vladimir Putin and President of Turkey, Recep Tayyip Erdogan, who is on a working visit to Russia, began at the Kremlin.
17 April 2019. Reports: The U.S. and Turkey have failed to break their impasse over Turkey's plan to deploy a Russian air defense system the Pentagon says could jeopardize U.S. fighter aircraft, including Lockheed Martin's F-35, which Turkish manufacturers helped build. Turkish officials repeated that the deal with Russia has been signed and is final, while the U.S. has threatened to impose sanctions under legislation that allows the punishment of entities doing business with Russia, and to expel Turkey from the F-35 program. The first batch of Russian S-400 missiles may be delivered as early as June, leaving little time for the dispute to be resolved.
30 April 2019. Vladimir Putin had a telephone conversation with President of the Republic of Turkey, Recep Tayyip Erdogan.

Greece: (Population 11.1 M, rank 82, decrease 0.2%. Free: 84 of 100).

Republic of North Macedonia: (Population 2 M, rank 147, growth 0.1%. Partly Free: 57 of 100).

Albania: (Population 2.9 M, rank 139, growth 0.1%. Partly free: 68 of 100).

Cyprus: (Population 1.1 M, rank 159, growth 0.8%. Free: 94 of 100). 26 April 2019. Vladimir Putin met with President of the Republic of Cyprus, Nicos Anastasiades, in Beijing, China.

Kazakhstan (Population 18.2 M, rank 64, growth 1.2%. Not free: 22 of 100. Area 2.72 M km^2, rank 9.).

Armenia: (Population 2.9 M, rank 138, growth 0.2%. Partly free: 45 of 100).

Azerbaijan: (Population 9.8 M, rank 90, growth 1.1%. Not free 14 of 100). 26 April 2019. Vladimir Putin met with President of the Republic of Azerbaijan, Ilham Aliyev, in Beijing, China.

Uzbekistan: (Population 31.9 M, rank 44, growth 1.5%. Not free: 3 of 100).

Kyrgyzstan (Population 6 M, rank 112, growth 1.5%. Partly free, 37 of 100).

Tajikistan: (Population 8.9 M, rank 96, growth 2.1%. Not free, 11 of 100).

Turkmenistan: (Population 5.7 M, rank 113, growth 1.7%. Not free, 4 of 100).

United Kingdom, Canada, South America

United Kingdom: (Population: 66.1 M, rank 21, growth 0.6%. Free: 95 of 100).

Ireland: (Population: 4.7 M, rank 123, growth 0.8%. Free: 96 of 100)

Canada: (Population: 36.6 M, rank 38, growth 0.9%. Free: 99 of 100. Area 9.9 M km^2, rank 2).
3 April 2019. Reports: MONTREAL, Quebec - Bombardier announced last week that its Global 7500 business jet recently added another record to its collection, as the Canada-based manufacturer flew from coast-to-coast, Los Angeles to New York, in just under four hours.
10 April 2019. Reports: Canada is "constantly looking at ways to refresh the [tariff] retaliation list [against the U.S.] to have an even greater impact," Foreign Minister Freeland told reporters, adding to the recent trade tensions taking place across the globe. David MacNaughton, Canada's ambassador to Washington, told U.S. agricultural reporters on Monday, 8 April, that Canada could announce a new list of targets as soon as next week, which would include a significant number of agricultural products.
- 2 May 2019. Reports: Pork is the next target of a widening conflict between China and Canada.

Iceland: (Population: 335,000, rank 180, growth 0.8%. Free 97 of 100).
10 April 2019. On the second day of the 5th International Arctic Forum "The Arctic: Territory of Dialogue", Vladimir Putin met in St. Petersburg, Russia, with President of the Republic of Iceland, Gudni Thorlacius Johannesson.

Mexico: (Population: 129.1 M, rank 10, growth 1.3%. Partly Free: 65 of 100. Area 1.96 M km^2, rank 13).

Chile: (Population: 18 M, rank 65, growth 0.8%. Free 94 of 100).

Colombia: (Population: 49 M, rank 29, growth 0.8%. Partly free 64 of 100).

Argentina: (Population: 44.2 M, rank 31, growth, 1%. Free: 82 of 100. Area 2.78 M km^2, rank 8.).

Brazil (Population: 209.2 M, rank 6, growth 0.8%. Free, 79 of 100. Area 8.5 M km^2, rank 5).

Peru: (Population: 32.1 M, rank 5, growth 1.2%. Free: 72 of 100)

Cuba: (Population: 11.4 M, rank 42, growth 0.1%. Not free, 15 of 100).

Bolivia: (Population: 11 M, rank 83, growth 1.5%. Partly free 68 of 100).

Paraguay: (Population: 6.8 M, rank 107, growth 1.3%. Partly free 64 of 100).

Panama: (Population: 4.1 M, rank 131, growth 1.6%. Free: 83 of 100).

Venezuela: (Population: 32 M, rank 43, growth 1.3%. Not free: 30 of 100).

Guyana: (Population 777K, (rank 165, grows 0.6%). Free: 74 of 100).

Trinidad and Tobago: (Population 1.3 M, (rank 153, grows 0.3%). Free: 81 of 100).

Nicaragua: (Population 6.2 M, (rank 110, grows 1.1%). Partly Free: 47 of 100).

El Salvador: (Population 6.3 M (rank 108, grows 0.5%). Free: 70 of 100).

France, Germany, and neighbors

France: (Population 64.9 M, rank 22, growth 0.4%. Free: 90 of 100).

Reports: 2019 is the 500th anniversary of the Renaissance in France's Loire Valley, which started in 1519.

16 April 2019. Vladimir Putin sent a message to President of the French Republic, Emmanuel Macron, personally expressing sympathy to the French leader, and the entire French nation, over the tragic aftermath of the fire at Notre Dame de Paris.

"Notre Dame is a historical symbol of France, a priceless treasure of European and world culture, one of the most important Christian shrines. The tragedy that occurred last night in Paris awoke an echo of pain in the hearts of Russians," the President of Russia wrote.

Vladimir Putin expressed the hope that the great cathedral can be restored, and offered to send to France the best Russian specialists with extensive experience in restoring world cultural heritage sites, including works of medieval architecture.

16 April 2019. Reports: Only minor injuries were sustained by the police and firemen during the hours-long fight to contain the flames at Notre Dame de Paris. Precious artifacts were saved, and President Macron has vowed to rebuild the cathedral. An international appeal to raise funds to rebuild is underway and, already, corporate leaders around the world have pledged hundreds of millions of dollars to restore the cathedral.

18 April 2019. Vladimir Putin met with top managers of leading French companies (Total, Renault, etc.).

16 April 2019. Reports: Airbus Helicopters has expanded its industrial footprint with the opening of the H135 final assembly line (FAL) in Qingdao. The factory is the first helicopter FAL built by a foreign manufacturer in China, as well as the first H135 FAL outside of Europe.

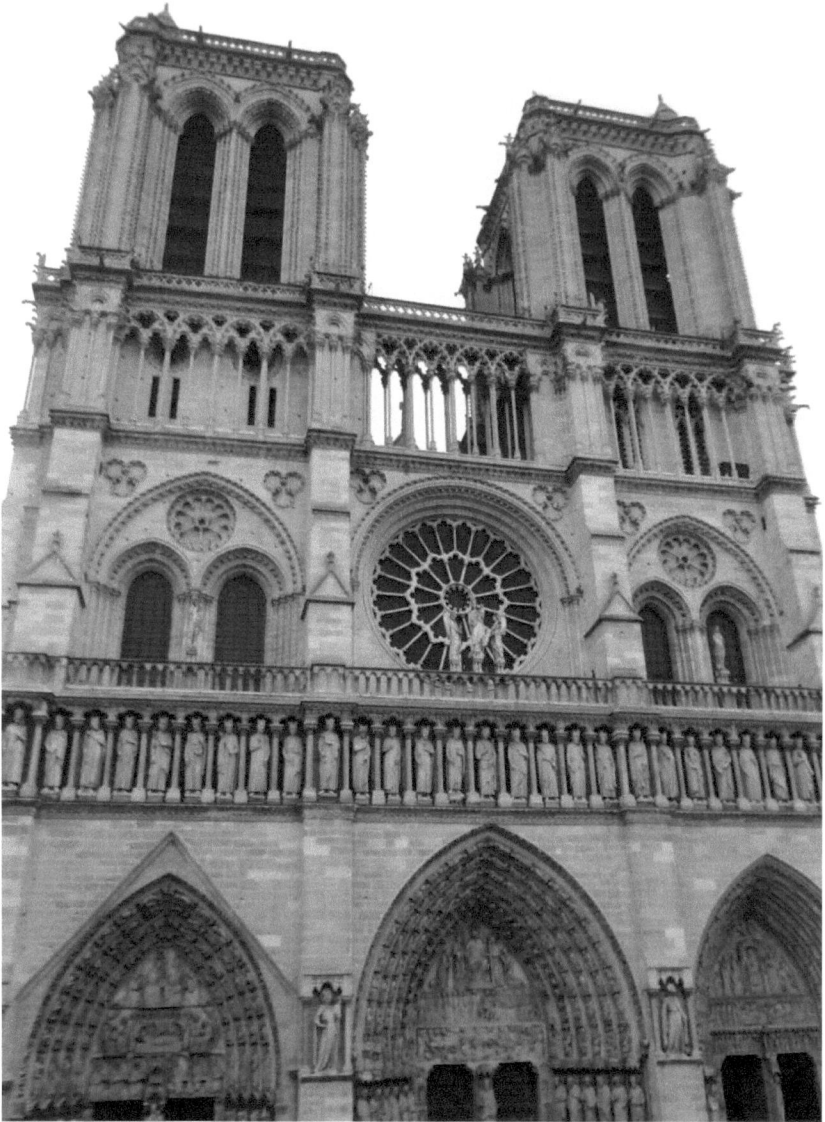

The upper part of the western façade of Cathédrale Notre Dame de Paris (1163 – 1345, 90 m), on the south-eastern part of the Île de la Cité, which is considered the center of Paris, in the fourth arrondissement. The organ has 7,374 pipes, with about 900 classified as historical. It has 110 real stops, five 56-key manuals and a 32-key pedalboard; it is now fully computerized. The Towers at Notre-Dame contain five church bells. The great bourdon bell, Emmanuel, from 1681, 13 t, is located in the South Tower (right).

Belgium (Population 11.4 M, rank 80, growth 0.6%. Free: 95 of 100).

European Commission, European Union, EU: 28 EU countries: Austria, Belgium, Bulgaria, Croatia, Republic of Cyprus, Czech Republic, Denmark, Estonia, Finland, France, Germany, Greece, Hungary, Ireland, Italy, Latvia, Lithuania, Luxembourg, Malta, Netherlands, Poland, Portugal, Romania, Slovakia, Slovenia, Spain, Sweden and the UK.

Germany: (Population 82.1 M, rank 16, growth 0.2%. Free: 95 of 100).

7 April 2019. During a telephone conversation, Vladimir Putin extended his warm wishes to retired Chancellor of the Federal Republic of Germany, Gerhard Schröder, on his 75th birthday.

Reports: STUTTGART, Germany - Late last month, the German Aerospace Center (DLR) held its E2Flight conference, where engineers, researchers, and those with a connection or interest in electric powered aircraft, gathered to discuss technology and engineering in the growing field.

18 April 2019. Vladimir Putin sent a message of condolences to President of the Federal Republic of Germany, Frank-Walter Steinmeier, and to Federal Chancellor, Angela Merkel, following the death of German citizens in a bus crush in Madeira (Portugal islands, 1,000 km southwest of Lisbon; 29 died, over 28 wounded).

Norway (Population 5.3 M, rank 118, growth 1%. Free: 100 of 100).

9 April 2019. Vladimir Putin met with Prime Minister of the Kingdom of Norway, Erna Solberg, on the sidelines of the 5th International Arctic Forum "The Arctic: Territory of Dialogue".

Sweden (Population 9.9 M, rank 89, growth 0.7%. Free: 100 of 100).

9 April 2019. The President of Russia met with Prime Minister of the Kingdom of Sweden, Stefan Löfven, on the sidelines of the 5th International Arctic Forum "The Arctic: Territory of Dialogue".

The Netherlands (Population 17 M, rank 67, growth 0.3%. Free: 99 of 100).

Czech Republic (Population 10.6 M, rank 87, growth 0.1%. Free: 94 of 100).

Denmark (Population 5.7 M, rank 114, growth 0.4%. Free: 97 of 100. Area (including Greenland) 2.22 M km^2, rank 12 but not official).

Luxembourg (Population 583 K, rank 169, growth 1.3%. Free: 98 of 100).

Spain: (Population 46.3 M, rank 30, growth 0%. Free: 94 of 100).

29 April 2019. Reports: For the third time in four years, Spaniards have elected a new government, and, although Prime Minister Pedro Sanchez will most probably remain in office, how he gets there is the key question. While a pact with liberals Ciudadanos would be seen as a positive for many observers, a partnership with anti-austerity party Podemos and Catalan pro-independence parties may be a less market-friendly option. Spain's Ibex 35 is only up 11% this year, making it one of Europe's worst performing stock indexes.

Portugal: (Population 10.3 M, rank 88, decrease 0.4%. Free: 97 of 100).

Liechtenstein: (Population: 38,000, rank 215, growth 0.7%, Free: 91 of 100)

India, Pakistan, Australia, and neighbors

India (Population: 1.3 B, rank 2nd, growth 1.1%. Free: 77 of 100. Area 3.28 M km^2, rank 7).

3 April 2019. Reports: NEW DELHI, India – Indian Prime Minister Narendra Modi said on March 27 that his country had successfully intercepted and destroyed a satellite in low-earth orbit. This first Indian anti-satellite test is militarily important.

10 April 2019. Reports: U.S. State Department approved sale of 24 MH-60R helicopters to India for anti-submarine warfare (ASW).

11 April 2019. Reports: Millions of Indian voters are heading to the polls in the first phase of the world's largest general election that's seen as a referendum on Prime Minister Narendra Modi. The seven-phase elections will conclude on May 19, with the party or coalition with a simple majority (273 seats) invited to form a government. The country faces high unemployment, sharpening sectarian and caste divisions, distress for rural farmers, and a recent flare-up with Pakistan.

Indonesia: (Population: 263.9 M, rank 4, growth 1.1%. Partly free: 65 of 100. Area 1.91 M km^2, rank 14.).

Australia: (Population: 24.4 M, rank 53, growth 1.3%. Free: 98 of 100. Area 7.69 M km^2, rank 6).
Reports: Australia government budget bolsters cyber security.

New Zealand: (Population 4.7 M, rank 125, growth 1%. Free: 98 of 100.

Pakistan: (Population 212 M, rank 5, growth 2%. Partly free: 43 of 100).

Philippines: (Population 104.9 M, rank 13, growth 1.5%. Partly free 63 of 100).

Singapore: (Population 5.7 M, rank 115, growth 1.5%. Partly free 51 of 100).

The EAS currently comprises 18 countries: 10 ASEAN members (Brunei Darussalam, Cambodia, Indonesia, Laos, Malaysia, Myanmar, the Philippines, Singapore, Thailand and Vietnam), and eight dialogue partners: Russia (joined the EAS in 2010), the United States, Japan, South Korea, India, China, Australia and New Zealand.

APEC (21 members: Singapore, China, USA, Vietnam, Australia, Japan, Indonesia, Russia, Philippines, Malaysia, Hong Kong, Thailand, Chile, Canada, New Zealand, South Korea, Peru, Mexico, Brunei, Papua New Guinea, Chinese Taipei)

Reports: Singapore is number 8 on the list of the world's healthiest countries.

Thailand: (Population 69 M, rank 20, growth 0.3%. Not free 32 of 100).

Myanmar (Burma, Population 53.3 M, rank 26, growth 0.9%. Not free 32 of 100. 26 April 2019. Vladimir Putin met with State Counsellor of the Republic of the Union of Myanmar, Aung San Suu Kyi, on the sidelines of the second Belt and Road Forum for International Cooperation, in Beijing, China.

Bangladesh (Population 164.6 M, rank 8, growth 1.1%. Partly free 47 of 100).

Sri Lanka (Population 20.8 M, rank 58, growth 0.4%. Partly free 56 of 100).

21 April 2019. Vladimir Putin sent condolences to Maithripala Sirisena, President of the Democratic Socialist Republic of Sri Lanka, in connection with the tragic consequences of a series of terrorist acts. A series of blasts tore through 3 churches and 4 international hotels in and around Colombo, as well as at Batticaloa, in east of Sri Lanka, on Easter morning, killing at least 207 people, and wounding more 450. Nearly all victims are Sri Lankan, with Dutch, Chinese, Portuguese and Turkish nationals also killed in attacks. The United States also condemned in the strongest terms the terrorist attacks in Sri Lanka on Easter morning.

Malaysia (Population 31.6 M, rank 45, growth 1.34%. Partly free 44 of 100).

Brunei: (Population 428,000, rank 176, growth 1.3%. Not free 29 of 100).

Vanuatu: (Population 276,000, rank 185, growth 2.2%. Free 80 of 100)

Tonga: (Population 108,000, rank 195, growth 0.8%. Free 74 of 100

Papua New Guinea: (Population 8.2 M, rank 101, growth 2.1%, Partly Free 64 of 100). APEC (21 members: Singapore, China, USA, Vietnam, Australia, Japan, Indonesia, Russia, Philippines, Malaysia, Hong Kong, Thailand, Chile, Canada, New Zealand, South Korea, Peru, Mexico, Brunei, Papua New Guinea, Chinese Taipei)

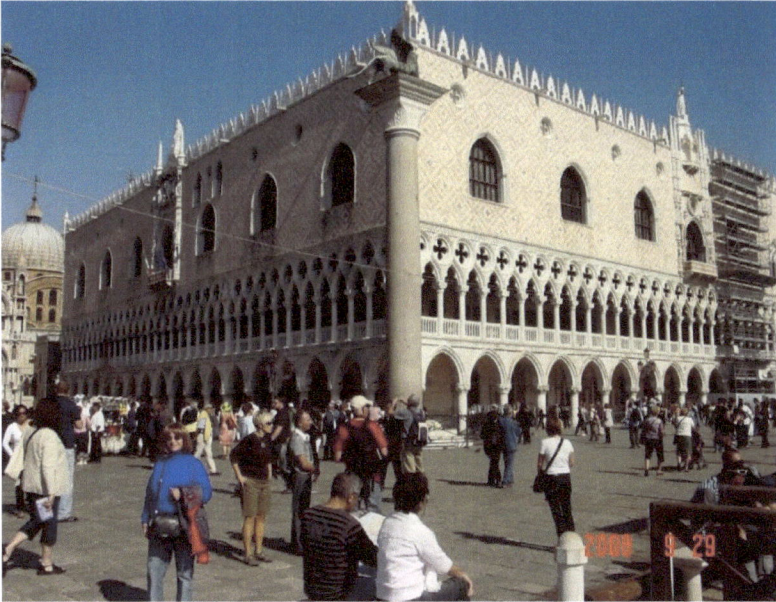

Italy, Venezia: 29 Sep 2008, Piazza San Marco (1084) looking northeast, Palazzo Ducale (1424), Basilica di San Marco (1173, left back), Column of the Lion (center, with the sculpture Lion of Venice on top),

Italy, Middle East, Africa

Italy: (Population 59.3 M, rank 23, decrease 0.1%. Free: 89 of 100).

10 April 2019. Reports: Italy's populist government has conceded it won't hit the budget-deficit target agreed on with EU authorities. The finance ministry said this year's deficit will be 2.4% of GDP, rather than 2% agreed upon in December after tense negotiations. Those discussions resulted in a rise in borrowing costs for Italian banks, businesses and households, reviving memories of the eurozone's 2010-12 debt crisis, from which Italy has yet to fully recover.

Vatican: (Population 792, rank 233 (last), decrease 1.1%).

San Marino: (Population 33,400, rank 218, growth 0.6%. Free 97 of 100)

Malta (Population 431,000, rank 175, growth 0.3%. Free, 96 of 100).

Jordan (Population 9.7 M, rank 92, growth 2.6%. Partly free, 37 of 100).

Lebanon: (Population: 6 M, rank 111, growth 1.3%. Partly free: 44 of 100).

United Arab Emirates (UAE) (Population: 9.4 M, rank 94, growth 1.4%. Not free, 20 of 100. Capital: Abu Dhabi. Dubai).

Reports: Amazon has launched a new Middle East marketplace, two years after buying the Dubai-based e-commerce company Souq.com for $580 M. With the launch, Amazon said Souq.com will be rebranded to Amazon.ae, although Souq remains available in Saudi Arabia and Egypt.

Saudi Arabia (Population 32.9 M, rank 41, growth 2.1%. Not free: 10 of 100. Area 2.149 M km^2, rank 12.).

Reports: Missile defense experts at Lockheed Martin Corp. will build missile defense rocket interceptors for the U.S. and Saudi Arabia, to protect against incoming ballistic missiles.

Yemen (Population 28.2 M, rank 50, growth 2.4%. Not free: 14 of 100).

Iraq (Population 38.2 M, rank 36, growth 2.9%. Not free: 27 of 100).

Iran: (Population 81.1 M, rank 18, growth 1.1%. Not free: 17 of 100).

Israel: (Population 8.3 M, rank 100, growth 1.6%. Free: 80 of 100).
4 April 2019. Vladimir Putin met at the Kremlin with Prime Minister of Israel, Benjamin Netanyahu, who has come to Russia on a brief working visit.

Palestine: (Population 4.9 M (rank 121, grows 2.7%). Not free: 28 of 100).

Egypt (Population 97.5 M (rank 14, grows 1.9%). Not free, 26 of 100). 26 April 2019. Vladimir Putin had a meeting with President of the Arab Republic of Egypt, Abdel Fattah el-Sisi, in Beijing, China.

League of Arab States (LAS) (22 countries: Algeria, Bahrein, Comoros, Djibouti, Egypt, Iraq, Jordan, Kuwait, Lebanon, Libya, Mauritania, Morocco, Oman, Palestine, Qatar, Saudi Arabia, Somalia, Sudan, Syria, Tunisia, United Arab Emirates and Yemen).
2 April 2019. Vladimir Putin sent his greetings to heads of state and government of the League of Arab States (LAS) member states on the opening of LAS Summit in Tunis, Tunisia.

Qatar: (Population 2.6 M (rank 142, grows 2.7%). Not free: 26 of 100).

Kuwait: (Population 4.1 M (rank 130, grows 2.1%). Partly free: 36 of 100).

Oman: (Population 4.6 M (rank 127, grows 4.8%). Not free: 25 of 100)

Bahrain: (Population 1.5 M (rank 152, grows 4.7%). Not free: 12 of 100).

Syria: (Population 18.2 M (rank 63, decrease 0.9%). Not free: 0 of 100).

Kenya: (Population 49.7 M (rank 28, growth 2.6%. Partly free, 51 of 100).

Libya: (Population 6.3 M, rank 109, growth 1.3%. Not free: 13 of 100).

Algeria: (Area 2.38 M km^2, rank 10.)

Tunisia: (Population 11.5 M, rank 78, growth 1.1%. Free: 78 of 100).

Morocco: (Population 35.7 M, rank 39, growth 1.3%. Partly free: 41 of 100).

South Africa: (Population 56.7 M, rank 25, growth 1.3%. Free, 78 of 100). 26 April 2019. Vladimir Putin expressed his condolences to President of the Republic of South Africa, Cyril Ramaphosa, on the tragic aftermath of floods and mudslides in the country's southeast.

Zimbabwe: (Population 16.5 M, rank 70, growth 2.4%. Partly Free, 32 of 100).

Sudan (Population 40.5 M, rank 35, growth 2.4%. Not Free: 6 of 100).

South Sudan (Population 12.5 M, rank 76, growth 2.8%. Not Free: 4 of 100)

Guinea: (Population 12.7 M, rank 75, growth 2.6%. Partly Free, 41 of 100).

Djibouti (Population 957,000, rank 160, growth 1.6%. Not Free: 26 of 100).

Somalia: (Population 14.7 M, rank 74, growth 3%. Not free: 5 of 100).

Niger (Population 21.4 M, rank 57, growth 3.9%. Partly free: 49 of 100).

Nigeria (Population 190.8 M, rank 7, growth 2.6%. Partly free: 50 of 100).

Cameroon (Population 24 M, rank 55, growth 2.6%. Not free: 24 of 100).

Sierra Leone: (Population 7.5 M (rank 103, grows 2.2%). Partly free: 66 of 100)

Chad: (Population 15 M (rank 73, grows 3.1%). Not free: 18 of 100).

The Gambia: (Population 2.1 M (rank 146, grows 3%). Not free: 20 of 100).

Malawi: (Population 18.6 M (rank 61, grows 2.9%). Partly free: 63 of 100).

Rwanda: (Population 12.2 M (rank 77, grows 2.4%). Not free: 24 of 100).

Burkina Faso: (Population 19.1 M (rank 60, grows 2.9%). Partly free: 63 of 100).

Central African Republic: (Population 4.6 M (rank 126, grows 1.4%). Not free: 10 of 100).

Senegal: (Population 15.8 M (rank 72, grows 2.8%). Free: 78 of 100).

Gabon: (Population 2 M (rank 149, grows 2.3%). Partly Free: 32 of 100).

Madagascar: (Population 25.5 M (rank 51, grows 2.7%). Partly Free: 56 of 100).

Democratic Republic of the Congo: (Population 81.3 M (rank 17, grows 3.3%). Not Free: 19 of 100. Area 2.34 M km^2, rank 11).

Angola: (Population 29.7 M (rank 46, grows 3.4%). Not Free: 24 of 100).
4 April 2019. Vladimir Putin held talks at the Kremlin with President of Angola, Joao Lourenco, who has come to Russia on an official visit.

Zambia: (Population 17 M (rank 66, grows 3%). Partly Free: 56 of 100).

United Republic of Tanzania: (Population 57 M (rank 24, grows 3.1%). Partly Free: 58 of 100).

Ethiopia: (Population 105 M (rank 12, grows 2.5%). Not Free: 12 of 100).

Japan, Kawaguchiko: 22 Nov 2008, the north side of Mount Fuji (3,776 m, 1707 last eruption) seen from 17 km north in Kawaguchi city, near Kawaguchiko (Lake Kawaguchi, 6 km^2, 830 m elevation, right), 100 km south-west of Tokyo.

Medical

Pharmaceutical companies are raising the prices of almost 3,000 drugs in the U.S. in the first three months of this year. Generic versions of the antidepressant Prozac, and the painkiller Vicodin, were among the medicines with triple-digit percentage increases. Drug costs continue to increase at four times the rate of inflation.

Through electronic health records, clinical trials, genomic sequencing, wearables, and medical devices, the healthcare industry generates great amounts of data. By leveraging this wealth of information, caregivers and researchers can improve diagnostics, accelerate medical research, develop personalized medicine, reduce costs, and more. But big data usage is lower in healthcare than in some other industries. Medical specialists are working to accelerate and optimize its use.

Consuming garlic helps counteract age-related changes in gut bacteria associated with memory problems, according to a new study conducted with mice. The benefit comes from allyl sulfide, a compound in garlic known for its health benefits. – Federation of American Societies for Experimental Biology (FASEB) Nutrition 2019, June 8-11, 2019

The hippocampus is the part of the brain responsible for memory, which naturally shrinks with the age.

Being in tune with the present moment -- called mindfulness -- can relieve stress.

A new study clearly shows that medication treatment reduces arrests among people with opioid use disorder. All criminal activities are due to sick people, who need special medical treatment in special locations – not prison, where they just learn new criminal activities, from people who are even sicker than themselves.

Researchers developed a treatment that turns tumors into cancer vaccine factories.

Reports: Taking a widely prescribed prostate cancer drug with a low-fat meal instead of on an empty stomach — the usual recommendation — can allow men to use a lower dose, with no loss in effectiveness, a 2018 study in the *Journal of Clinical Oncology* finds. Abiraterone (Zytiga) is approved for the treatment of metastatic castration-resistant prostate cancer (M-CRPC), meaning cancer that has spread beyond the prostate, and no longer responds to androgen deprivation therapy. The approved dose is 1,000 mg daily, with no food consumed for at least two hours before, or for an hour after, taking it. Some studies had shown that taking abiraterone with food significantly increased concentrations of the drug in the body. With that in mind, researchers randomly assigned 68 men with M-CRPC to take 250 mg of abiraterone daily along with a low-fat breakfast, or to take the usual dose on an empty stomach at least two hours before breakfast. At 12 weeks, the low dose of abiraterone taken with food was slightly more effective than the higher-dose empty-stomach regimen, as measured by decreases in PSA levels. Moreover, both doses staved off progression of cancer the same length of time, roughly nine months. Abiraterone costs about $10,000 a month, and many men take it for several years. A lower dose taken with food could mean smaller co-payments and more convenience for the men who take it.

A new updated ISO 10993-1 standard came out in August of 2018 that drastically changed how we access medical devices for biocompatibility. We're also dealing with the impact of the Medical Device Regulations in Europe. The timing of these two documents has greatly disrupted the medical device industry.

Johns Hopkins Kimmel Cancer Center researchers say a new study of clusters of mouse cells known as "organoids" has significantly strengthened evidence that epigenetic changes, common to aging, play an essential role in colon cancer initiation.
– Johns Hopkins Medicine, Cancer Cell

Cancer-killing combination therapies were unveiled with new drug-screening tool.

FDA approved a new treatment for osteoporosis in postmenopausal women.

Researchers developed a new recombinant vaccine called NIPRAB that shows robust immunization against Nipah virus in animal models, and may be effective against other viruses in the same family. – Thomas Jefferson University, Vaccines

Doctors recommend for elderly to plan with family members their medical issues, and especially to find sustainable and smart ideas for ageing well.

Researchers have discovered that the spatial organization of the genome can be altered using small molecule compounds, which are considered as promising anti-cancer drugs.

Medical specialists observed that precise decoding of breast cancer cells created new option for treatment.

Researchers have completed the largest analysis of a new gene fusion they believe is responsible for development of a wide spectrum of cancer types.

A new clinical trial shows that a drug lowers the risk of kidney failure by a third in people with Type 2 diabetes and kidney disease.

Screen time above a two-hour threshold, at five years of age, is associated with an increased risk of clinically relevant externalizing problems, such as inattention, according to a study published on April 17.

One negative behavior, such as substance abuse or heavy alcohol drinking, can lead college students toward a vicious cycle of poor lifestyle choices, lack of sleep, mental distress, and low grades, according to new research from Binghamton University. State University of New York.
Trends in Neuroscience and Education, March-2019.

DNA is just an inert blueprint for life. It is the ribosome — an ancient and enormous molecular machine made up of half a million atoms — that makes DNA come to life, by turning the genetic code into proteins, and therefore into people.

Each year in the world there are 131.4 M of births (4.16/second), and 55.3 M people die (1.754/second). About half of the world's deaths are the result of medical emergencies.

Scientists create first-ever added manufacturing heart.

Study highlights anti-tumor activity of curcumin on stomach cancer.

A new wearable sensor monitors health through sweat, using nanotech.

In a new study, Yale Cancer Center scientists have demonstrated a powerful method to analyze how tumor cells are altered as they metastasize to the brain. This method may improve the detection and treatment of the advanced brain cancer.
– Cell Reports

A mathematical model of a small animal regeneration starts to answer the question – what signals determine the rebuilding of specific anatomical structures in regeneration? The model predicts and confirms factors determining body pattern formation, showing a new role for the nervous system in regeneration.
– Tufts University, PLOS Computational Biology 26-Apr-2019

Protein manipulation could be the key to treating ALS (Amyotrophic Lateral Sclerosis), and frontotemporal dementia.

Researchers found that nanomaterial helps heal damage after a heart attack.

Tumor-selective angiotensin blockers may improve response to cancer immunotherapy.

In a study published on 30 April in the journal PLOS Biology, researchers at Penn Medicine identify the mechanisms behind tumor growth following circadian disturbances, and show cancer treatment may be more effective at specific times of day.
– Perelman School of Medicine at the University of Pennsylvania
PLOS Biology / April 2019

An open-label, multi-cohort Phase II trial, led by investigators at The University of Texas M. D. Anderson Cancer Center, reports that treatment with the drug tagraxofusp resulted in high response rates (90%) in patients with deadly blood cancer, with no prior available therapies. New England Journal of Medicine

Restrictive prior authorization obstacles cause unnecessary delays and interference in care decisions for cancer patients, according to a new survey of nearly 700 radiation oncologists — physicians who treat cancer patients using radiation.
– American Society for Radiation Oncology (ASTRO)

Biomarker for the chronic fatigue syndrome was identified by scientists.

Capsaicin, the compound responsible for chili peppers' heat, slowed the progression of lung cancer in cell cultures and animal models.

People who don't give up on their goals (or who get better over time at not giving up on their goals), and who have a positive outlook, appear to have less anxiety and depression and fewer panic attacks, according to a study of thousands of Americans. – American Psychological Association (APA), Journal of Abnormal Psychology

The results of a research identified a specific nook in the SET protein's shape that provides a snug fit for ceramide, used for cancer therapies.

A drug commonly used to treat multiple sclerosis may, after necessary modifications, one day be used to treat patients with epilepsy.

Scientists at Seattle Children's Research Institute are paving the way to use gene-edited B cells – a type of white blood cell in the immune system – to treat a wide range of potential diseases that affect children, including hemophilia. – Seattle Children's Hospital

Reports: The U.S. has the biggest outbreak of measles in 25 years. The CDC reported 704 cases of measles as of April 26, a 1.3% increase since the 695 reported the week before, with the vast majority of cases occurring in children who have not received the MMR vaccine.

Switzerland, Lausanne (Roman 150, 147,000, 41 km^2, 500 m elevation, 62 km northeast of Geneva, the home of the International Olympic Committee), near Château d'Ouchy (1170, 1609, 1893).

Mathematics, Science & Artificial Intelligence (AI)

The essential stage every battery needs to undergo in the manufacturing process is battery formation. Formation cycling has great impact on battery lifetime, quality and cost, but is currently the bottleneck in the production process.

Textile waste is a worldwide problem and textile recycling has increased dramatically, but there is still a large area for improvement, because waste and costs can be reduced, and recycled materials can more closely mimic the original virgin material. Specialists are working on new ideas for processes of textile materials, such that these textile materials are more easily deconstructed during recycling, the quality of the recycle is improved, and total costs of recycling are reduced.

Specialists are looking for reversible exothermic reaction chemistries that can be used in different applications at cold temperature (0 - 30 degrees C), to quickly heat up lubricants and lower their viscosity.

In order to significantly slow down or stop oxidation of lubricating oils, engineers are looking for compounds that can decompose or inactivate nitrate esters, without producing free radicals or unstable products.

Engineers are interested in technical designs of electric vehicle (EV) charging stations that are easily accessible, with minimal visual and physical impact within an urban environment.

4 April 2019. Reports: Verizon has launched 5G wireless service in parts of Chicago and Minneapolis, while carriers in South Korea - SK Telecom and KT Corp. - deployed their service in the Seoul metropolitan area. To access the network, Verizon subscribers for now will be limited to the Motorola Z3 (with an accessory clip-

on), while Korean early adopters will have to use Samsung's Galaxy S10.

Mathematics and Computer Science teacher shortages are major problems in the U.S. and other countries.

Researchers are analyzing the quality implications of continuous manufacturing.

Specialists want to make English text and speech readily understandable to computers, by creating an artificial intelligence (AI) prototype that can learn language in much the same way as a young child does -- from visual and auditory cues.

Reports: Mercury Systems Inc. in Andover, Mass., is introducing an embedded computing blade server, with hardware-enabled support for artificial intelligence (AI) applications.

The very sophisticated computational fluid dynamics can be applied to the analysis of a minienvironment cleanroom.

Americans used more energy in 2018 than in any other year, according to the most recent energy flow charts released by Lawrence Livermore National Laboratory. Overall total energy consumption rose to 101.2 quadrillion BTU. Again, it is very clear for many years that the change of time is just another government imposed wrong decision, which should be eliminated.

Robots need more than just artificial intelligence (AI) to be autonomous. They need a lot of sensors, sensor fusion, and real-time inference at the edge.

IBM helped NASA fix one of its satellites, which is on a geosynchronous equatorial orbit (GEO, or geostationary orbit (the circular geosynchronous orbit could be outside the equatorial plane – there are 402 such satelites) at 35,786 km above Earth, orbital velocity 3.07 km/s, orbital period 1,436 minutes = 23.934461223 hours (almost exactly one sidereal day)), using cutting-edge deep learning artificial intelligence (AI).

Researchers are working to develop real time machine learning hardware able to interpret and learn from data, solve unfamiliar problems using what it has learned, and operate at power levels on par or better than the human brain.

There is intense mathematical research in the area of AI applications in medical imaging.

Bird strikes by aircraft need to be addressed quickly for safety. Identification of the bird is critical to determine its size and weight, and to determine if more testing for damage is required and what action to take. Currently, birds can be identified by DNA and feather identification, but the methods are time consuming (weeks) including shipping samples back and forth. Researchers are working on a faster method for bird identification, preferably with a handheld device.

Superinjection, the effect used in lasers and LEDs creation, can work in "pure" semiconductors, which was previously considered impossible. This opens up new prospects for designing highly efficient blue, violet, ultraviolet, and white LEDs.
– Moscow Institute of Physics and Technology (MIPT)
Semiconductor Science and Technology

Reports: Almost 50 years man first walked on the Moon, and now a few countries are again preparing to land on the Earth's satellite. This year China has landed a robotic spacecraft on the far side of the moon, and NASA has announced it wants to send astronauts to the Moon's south pole by 2024. On July 21, 1969, the Apollo 11 crew installed the first set of mirrors to reflect lasers targeted at the Moon from Earth. The subsequent experiments, carried out using these arrays, have helped scientists to work out the distance between the Earth and Moon for the past 50 years. We now know that the Moon's orbit has been getting larger by 3.8 cm per year — it is moving away from the Earth. This distance, and the use of Moon rocks to date the Moon's formation to 4.51 billions of years ago, are the basis for the giant impact hypothesis (the theory that the Moon formed from debris after a collision early in Earth's history).

The loss of tidal energy (due to friction between the moving ocean and the seabed) slows the planet's spin, which forces the Moon to move away from it. The detailed mathematics that describe this evolution were first developed by George Darwin, son of the great Charles Darwin, in 1880. It is important to try to detect Milankovitch cycles from physical and chemical changes in ancient sediments. These cycles come about because of variations in the shape and orientation of Earth's orbit, and variations in the orientation of Earth's axis. These produced climate cycles, such as the ice ages, and the subsequent warmings, of the last few millions of years. Sediments from China suggest that 1.4 billions of years ago the Earth-Moon distance was 341,000 km (its current distance is 384,000 km).

Many believe that great scientists are most creative when they're young, but this is not true. A new study of winners of the Nobel Prize in economics finds that there are two different life cycles of creativity, one that shows up when scientists are young, and the other one – when they mature. – Ohio State University De Economist

H3N2 viruses mutate during vaccine production, but new technology could fix it.

A new updated ISO 10993-1 standard came out in August of 2018 that drastically changed how the medical devices are accessed for biocompatibility.

Since it was first widely used as a Leyden jar in 1748, three years after its invention in 1745, the battery hasn't changed — but its applications have.

Researchers are working to develop enabling technologies for insect-size robots, able to perform complex jobs, like disaster relief, or inspecting hazardous environments that are inaccessible to larger robots.

Microencapsulation is a technique in which substances are coated to form extremely small capsules. These particles are used in many industries for the delivery of materials, such as vitamins, minerals, and pharmaceuticals. Scientists are working on methods for improving the stability of microcapsules in aqueous solutions, and for controlled slow release of small molecules.

Chemists are working on reversible exothermic reaction chemistries that can be used in different applications at cold temperature (0-30° C), to quickly heat up lubricants, and lower their viscosity.

Italy, Udine: 3 November 2009, from Piazza della Liberta, going to the northwest corner and passing under Arco Bollani, we are on the slope (looking northeast) to Castello (983, 1517-1567, 138 m, left up) di Udine, now hosting the History and Art Museum of Udine.

General news and issues

Reports: Advertisers are shifting from Google to Amazon – WSJ. But more customers complain about ads on top of everything – they search for a list of books, but now, on top, they get an ad for another book. Is the search algorithm wrong? Or some uninspired sales rep forced an ad on top? Not being customer friendly is not recommended.

Reports: Jeff Bezos is seen as essential to Amazon's meteoric growth, and stock price rise, since he founded the company as an online bookseller 25 years ago, in 1994.

The cybercriminals, not being arrested, continue their criminal activities: they were stilling data using exfiltration from a previously attacked and illegally infiltrated security camera at an investment firm in Japan. They attacked, using a zero-day trojan, a manufacturing company's network. Cybercriminals daily attack many companies and people using highly targeted spear phishing campaigns.

In the first half of 2018, the cybercriminals did 2.8 M DDoS attacks on organizations around the world. The attackers are getting more innovative, the attacks are getting bigger.

Over the last year we have seen a dramatic rise in the number of cybercriminals' attacks to steal data.

The people everywhere are asking the authorities to arrest the cybercriminals.

Reports: it is well known that the governments many times harm the prudent and civilized through the subsidization of the imprudent and uncivilized.

As we all know, money is, obviously, better left in the hands of the people than the government.

Reports: COLORADO SPRINGS, Colo. - The U.S. Air Force Life Cycle Management Center, and a consortium of tech firms led by Raytheon, are modernizing and simplifying the legacy

Space Defense Operations Center, a 1990s-era system that tracks and monitors space debris.

Reports: In oral arguments before the U.S. Supreme Court last fall, the justices struggled with an apparently absurd question: Should lawyers be able to earn a fee for negotiating a settlement that pays their clients nothing? The truth is that, because of the exorbitant lawyers' fees, very often people cannot go to court to ask for corrections of abuses – therefore the rule of law cannot be applied – simply, for over 70% of the population, there is no justice!

Conversation with the Sun:
The Sun: I made you all long ago, I see you all (even when you don't see me), and you are all sick!
I: Why?
The Sun: You all spend so much money, energy and time to build complicated staff to kill each other, instead of doing useful things for each other.
I: Yes, but we want to defend ourselves.
The Sun: Friend, the best defense is to talk to each other, until you find a good balance. More arms are not helping to defend, they just increase the danger of a catastrophic war – this is what you all want??
I: Not really….
The Sun: Then start talking, with calm and politeness, until you reach good agreements for the people, not for the personal ambitions of some leaders. It is not easy, but it is much better than preparing for a catastrophic war. Don't respond, just be healthy and smart, please!

12 April 2019. Reports: The most powerful operational rocket in the world, SpaceX's Falcon Heavy, launched its first commercial mission yesterday evening, 11 April, with all three boosters returning to Earth. At a price of $90 M per launch, it's also about a third of the cost of its closest competitor, United Launch Alliance's, Delta IV Heavy.

12 April 2019. Reports: The retail industry has issued a response to yesterday's challenge from Jeff Bezos, which dared

Amazon's top competitors to "match our employee benefits and our $15 minimum wage." "How about paying your taxes?" declared Walmart's Dan Bartlett, stating Amazon paid $0 in federal taxes on more than $11 B in profits last year. "We decided to put [tax savings] back into the community of our colleagues," Macy's CEO Jeffrey Gennette added, while eBay CEO Devin Wenig responded back, saying, "we don't compete with our sellers. We don't bundle endless services to create barriers to competition."

Reports: Rep. Thomas Massie, like many others, clarified again some issues regarding the frequent false climate alarms, which are based on incorrect data.

Reports: Amazon's new investments in air cargo transport companies indicate interest in the development of its own third-party carrier service.

Comcast and T-Mobile launched anti-robocalling feature. There are many requests that Verizon and AT&T also block robocalling.

French retailer Casino is expanding its partnership with online commerce giant Amazon to add Amazon lockers at 1,000 of its stores in France, and make Casino-branded products available on Amazon's website and app. The upscale Monoprix-brand products will also be available to Amazon Prime Now customers outside of Paris.

Reports: Millions of people are unhappy with the computer services they receive – bad service, bad e-mail (many times not working), and everything very expensive. People ask for an office where to report all these problems, and an inspector from this office should help the people.

Amazon reported Q1 results that beat earnings per share estimates by a hefty $2.44, and met revenue estimates with 17% Y/Y growth. But sluggish retail sales overseas, and a flat performance from Whole Foods, weighed down revenue growth for a fourth straight quarter. Amazon's operating margin climbed to 7.4% in the quarter, as expenses rose 12.6%, the lowest percentage gain in at least a decade. Expenses likely will move higher, in part because Amazon said it will invest $800 M to make one-day free shipping the new standard for core Prime members.

Reports: Amazon may be cutting at Google's dominance in digital advertising. It also has the upper hand in cluster (sometimes wrongly called cloud) computing (AWS), voice-activated devices (Alexa), and some 54% of people looking for a product now begin their search directly on Amazon.com.

Reports: Amazon's disclosure during its earnings call: it plans to roll out one-day Prime shipping this year through what's anticipated to be a heavy investment in the company's in-house delivery infrastructure.

New York: Times Square: 7th Ave (right straight), Broadway (center straight), W 43rd St (left and right), Marriott Marquis (right), Bertelsmann Building (left), Conde Nast Building (next), looking south.

Humor

The beautiful summer ends, and the schools begin.
The teacher:
- You had a nice vacation, and the summer passed so fast….
A little boy from the back:
- It should get a speeding ticket!

France, Paris: A Lamborghini supercar (Automobili Lamborghini, 1963, Italy), in the east part of Place de la Concorde, near Tuileries Gardens – no speeding ticket yet…..

Universe Axioms

Formulated by Michael M. Dediu

The following axioms are not independent of each other. They express in different ways the same concept of infinity.

Axiom 1. Pointing a theoretical laser from Earth, in any direction, at any time, after a finite amount of time the laser beam will touch an astronomic body.

Axiom 2. In any direction in space starting from Earth, at any time, there is an astronomic body from which the Earth can be theoretically seen.

Axiom 3. Infinity of space: Any straight line passing through the Earth's center intersects an infinite number of astronomic bodies.

Axiom 4. Infinity of time: Representing the time on a line, with the origin at the beginning of the year 1, the time goes to infinite in both positive and negative directions.

Axiom 5. Infinity of life: Because of the infinity of space and time, it is normal to consider that the life exists at any time, in an infinite number of places. Therefore right now, when you are reading this book, there is life outside the Earth, in an infinite number of places, but we do not know yet how to contact them.

Axiom 6. The Earth rotates itself around its polar axis, the Moon and many artificial satellites rotate around the Earth, in the Solar System all the planets and many other objects rotate around the Sun, the Solar System itself rotates around the center of the Milky Way galaxy, the Milky Way galaxy and all the billions of galaxies in our Universe (denoted U_1) rotate around the center of our Universe U_1, our Universe U_1, together with billions of other similar Universes, are inside a bigger Universe U_2 and rotate around the center of U_2, then U_2 and many others like it are inside a bigger U_3 and rotate around the center of U_3, and so on. Therefore, in general, the Universe U_n together with many similar Universes are inside the bigger Universe U_{n+1} and rotate around the center of U_{n+1}, for any n natural number, which goes to infinity. This can be written in the formula:

$$U_1 \subset U_2 \subset U_3 \subset \ldots \subset U_n \subset U_{n+1} \subset \ldots, \text{ n natural number.}$$

UK, Oxford, Oriel College (1326, in the east range of First quadrangle, the ornate portico in the center, with the inscription Regnante Carolo).

Time Axioms

Formulated by Michael M. Dediu

Axiom 1. Time is the most important force in the Univers.

Axiom 2. Everything is a function of time.

Axiom 3. Time exists in absolutely everything.

Axiom 4. Time creates and distroys everything.

Axiom 5. Time is invisible, inodor, insipid, unpalpabil, unaudible, but exists evrywhere.

Axiom 6. There are infinitezimal time particles, without mass, which are present everywhere, and which actually continuously transform everything.

UK, Cambridge, From Trinity Lane looking south to the west part of the northern façade and entrance of King's College Chapel (1446).

Bibliography

"The Histories" by Polybius
"Discours de la Méthode" by René Descartes
"Meditationes de prima philosophia" by René Descartes
"Philosophiae Naturalis Principia Mathematica" by Isaac Newton
Chinese encyclopedia Gujin Tushu Jicheng (Imperial Encyclopedia)
"Encyclopédie" by Jean-Baptiste le Rond d'Alembert and Denis Diderot
"Encyclopaedia Britannica" by over 4,400 contributors
"Encyclopedia Americana" by Francis Lieber

Michael M. Dediu is also the author of these books (which can be found on Amazon.com, and www.derc.com):

1. Aphorisms and quotations – with examples and explanations
2. Axioms, aphorisms and quotations – with examples and explanations
3. 100 Great Personalities and their Quotations
4. Professor Petre P. Teodorescu – A Great Mathematician and Engineer
5. Professor Ioan Goia – A Dedicated Engineering Professor
6. Venice (Venezia) – a new perspective. A short presentation with photographs
7. La Serenissima (Venice) - a new photographic perspective. A short presentation with many photos
8. Grand Canal – Venice. A new photographic viewpoint. A short presentation with many photos
9. Piazza San Marco – Venice. A different photographic view. A short presentation with many photos
10. Roma (Rome) - La Città Eterna. A new photographic view. A short presentation with many photos
11. Why is Rome so Fascinating? A short presentation with many photos
12. Rome, Boston and Helsinki. A short photographic presentation
13. Rome and Tokyo – two captivating cities. A short photographic presentation
14. Beautiful Places on Earth – A new photographic presentation

15. From Niagara Falls to Mount Fuji via Rome - A novel photographic presentation

16. From the USA and Canada to Italy and Japan - A fresh photographic presentation

17. Paris – Why So Many Call This City Mon Amour - A lovely photographic presentation

18. The City of Light – Paris (La Ville-Lumière) - A kaleidoscopic photographic presentation

19. Paris (Lutetia Parisiorum) – the romance capital of the world - A kaleidoscopic photographic view

20. Paris and Tokyo – a joyful photographic presentation. With a preamble about the Universe

21. From USA to Japan via Canada – A cheerful photographic documentary

22. 200 Wonderful Places, In The Last 50 Years – A personal photographic documentary

23. Must see places in USA and Japan - A kaleidoscopic photographic documentary

24. Grandeurs of the World - A kaleidoscopic photographic documentary

25. Corneliu Leu – writer on the same wavelength as Mark Twain. An American viewpoint

26. From Berkeley to Pompeii via Rome – A kaleidoscopic photographic documentary

27. From America to Europe via Japan - A kaleidoscopic photographic documentary

28. Discover America and Japan - A photographic documentary

29. J. R. Lucas – philosopher on a creative parallel with Plato, An American viewpoint

30. From America to Switzerland via France - A photographic documentary

31. From Bretton Woods to New York via Cape Cod - A photographic documentary

32. Splendid Places on the Atlantic Coast of the U. S. A. - A photographic documentary

33. Fourteen nice Cities on three Continents - A photographic documentary

34. 17 Picturesque Cities on the World Map - A photographic documentary

35. Unforgettable Places from Four Continents, including Trump buildings - A photographic documentary

36. Dediu Newsletter, Volume 1, Number 1, 6 December 2016 – Monthly news, review, comments and suggestions for a better and wiser world

37. Dediu Newsletter, Volume 1, Number 2, 6 January 2017 (available also at www.derc.com).

38. Dediu Newsletter, Volume 1, Number 3, 6 February 2017 (available at www.derc.com).

39. London and Greenwich, - A photographic documentary

40. Dediu Newsletter, Volume 1, Number 4, 6 March 2017 (available also at www.derc.com).

41. Dediu Newsletter, Volume 1, Number 5, 6 April 2017 (available also at www.derc.com).

42. Dediu Newsletter, Volume 1, Number 6, 6 May 2017 (available also at www.derc.com).

43. Dediu Newsletter, Volume 1, Number 7, 6 June 2017 (available also at www.derc.com).

44. London, Oxford and Cambridge, A photographic documentary

45. Dediu Newsletter, Volume 1, Number 8, 6 July 2017 (available also at www.derc.com).

46. Dediu Newsletter, Volume 1, Number 9, 6 August 2017 (available also at www.derc.com).

47. Dediu Newsletter, Volume 1, Number 10, 6 September 2017 (available also at www.derc.com).

48. Three Great Professors: President Woodrow Wilson, Historian German Arciniegas, and Mathematician Gheorghe Vranceanu – A chronological and photographic documentary

49. Dediu Newsletter, Volume 1, Number 11, 6 October 2017 (available also at www.derc.com).

50. Dediu Newsletter, Volume 1, Number 12, 6 November 2017 (available also at www.derc.com).

51. Dediu Newsletter, Volume 2, Number 1 (13), 6 December 2017 (available also at www.derc.com).

52. Two Great Leaders: Augustus and George Washington - A chronological and photographic documentary

53. Dediu Newsletter, Volume 2, Number 2 (14), 6 January 2018 (available also at www.derc.com).

54. Newton, Benjamin Franklin, and Gauss, A chronological and photographic documentary

55. Dediu Newsletter, Volume 2, Number 3 (15), 6 February 2018 (available also at www.derc.com).

56. 2017: World Top Events, But Many Little Known, A chronological and photographic documentary

57. Dediu Newsletter, Volume 2, Number 4 (16), 6 March 2018 (available also at www.derc.com).

58. Vergilius, Horatius, Ovidius, and Shakespeare - A chronological and photographic documentary.

59. Dediu Newsletter, Volume 2, Number 5 (17), 6 April 2018 (available also at www.derc.com).

60. Dediu Newsletter, Volume 2, Number 6 (18), 6 May 2018 (available also at www.derc.com).

61. Vivaldi, Bach, Mozart, and Verdi - A chronological and photographic documentary.

62. Dediu Newsletter, Volume 2, Number 7 (19), 6 June 2018 (available also at www.derc.com).

63. Dediu Newsletter, Volume 2, Number 8 (20), 6 July 2018 (available also at www.derc.com).

64. Dediu Newsletter, Volume 2, Number 9 (21), 6 August 2018 (available also at www.derc.com).

65. World History, a new perspective - A chronological and photographic documentary.

66. World Humor History with over 100 Jokes, a new perspective - A chronological and photographic documentary

67. Dediu Newsletter, Volume 2, Number 10 (22), 6 September 2018 (available also at www.derc.com).

68. Dediu Newsletter, Volume 2, Number 11 (23), 6 October 2018 (available also at www.derc.com).

69. Dediu Newsletter, Volume 2, Number 12 (24), 6 November 2018

70. Da Vinci, Michelangelo, Rembrandt, Rodin - A chronological and photographic documentary

71. Dediu Newsletter, Volume 3, Number 1 (25), 6 December 2018

72. Dediu Newsletter, Volume 3, Number 2 (26), 6 January 2019

73. From Euclid to Edison – revelries in the past 75 years - A chronological and photographic documentary

74. – Socrates to Churchill Aphorisms celebrated after 1960 - A chronological and photographic documentary
75. - Dediu Newsletter, Volume 3, Number 3 (27), 6 February 2019
76. – Hippocrates to Fleming: Medicine History celebrated after 1943 - A chronological and photographic documentary
77. - Dediu Newsletter, Volume 3, Number 4 (28), 6 March 2019
78. - Dediu Newsletter, Volume 3, Number 5 (29), 6 April 2019

New York: On 5th Ave, the southeast façade of the New York Public Library, 1902.

Mathematical research papers published in international mathematical journals

1. Dediu, M. On the lens spaces. *Rev. Roumaine Math. Pures Appl.* **14** (1969) 623-627.

2. Dediu, M. Sur quelques propriétés des espaces lenticulaires. (French) *Rev. Roumaine Math. Pures Appl.* **17** (1972), 871-874.

3. Vranceanu, G; Dediu, M. Tangent vector fields in projective spaces V_3 and in the lens spaces $L^3(3)$. (Romanian) Stud. Cerc. Mat. **24** (1972), 1585-1600.

4. Dediu, M. Tangent vector fields on lens spaces of dimension three (Italian) *Atti Accad. Naz. Lincei Rend. Cl. Sci. Fis. Mat. Natur.* **54** (1974), no. 2, 329-334 (1977

5. Dediu, M. Campi di vettori tangenti sullo spazio lenticolare $L^7(3)$. (Italian) *Atti Accad. Naz. Lincei Rend. Cl. Sci. Fis. Mat. Natur. (8)* **58** (1975), no. 1, 14-17.

6. Dediu, M. Tre campi di vettori tangenti indepedenti sugli spazi lenticolari di dimensione 4n+3. (Italian) *Atti Accad. Naz. Lincei Rend. Cl. Sci. Fis. Mat. Natur. (8)* **58** (1975), no. 2, 174-178.

7. Dediu, M. Sopra la metrica Vranceanu generalizzata (Italian) *Atti Accad. Naz. Lincei Rend. Cl. Sci. Fis. Mat. Natur. (8)* **58** (1975), no.3, 354-359).

8. Dediu, M. Sopra la metrica Vranceanu generalizzata (Italian) *Atti Accad. Naz. Lincei Rend. Cl. Sci. Fis. Mat. Natur. (8)* **58** (1975), no.3, 354-359).

9. Dediu, S.; Dediu, M. Sopra gli spazi proiettivi. *Rend. Sem. Fac. Sci. Univ. Cagliari* **46** (1976), suppl., 149-152.

10. Dediu, M.; Caddeo, Renzo; Dediu Sofia Alcune proprietà di una superficie immersa in uno spazio di Hilbert. (Italian) *Rend. Ist. Mat. Univ. Trieste* **8** (1976), no. 2, 147-161 (1977)

11. Dediu, S.; Dediu, M.; Caddeo, R. Alcune proprietà della metrica di Vranceanu generalizzata. (Italian) *Rend Sem. Fac. Sci. Univ Cagliari* **46** (1976), suppl., 153-161.

12. Dediu, Sofia; Dediu, M.; Caddeo, Renzo The Vrănceanu metric in local coordinates. (Italian) *Atti Accad. Sci. Lett. Arti Palermo Parte I (4)* **37** (1977/78). 331-339 (1980)

13. Dediu, M.; Caddeo, Renzo; Dediu, Sofia The extension of an *E*-premanifold to an *E*-manifold. (Italian) *Rend. Circ. Mat. Palermo (2)* **27** (1978), no. 3, 353-358.

France, Paris: L'Arc de Triomphe de l'Étoile (1836, 50 m), in the center of the Place Charles de Gaulle (1890-1970), seen from Champs-Élysées.

Michael M. Dediu is the editor of these books (also on Amazon.com, and www.derc.com):

1. Sophia Dediu: The life and its torrents – Ana. In Europe around 1920
2. Proceedings of the 4th International Conference "Advanced Composite Materials Engineering" COMAT 2012
3. Adolf Shvedchikov: I am an eternal child of spring – poems in English, Italian, French, German, Spanish and Russian
4. Adolf Shvedchikov: Life's Enigma – poems in English, Italian and Russian
5. Adolf Shvedchikov: Everyone wants to be HAPPY – poems in English, Spanish and Russian
6. Adolf Shvedchikov: My Life, My Love – poems in English, Italian and Russian
7. Adolf Shvedchikov: I am the gardener of love – poems in English and Russian
8. Adolf Shvedchikov: Amaretta di Saronno – poems in English and Russian
9. Adolf Shvedchikov: A Russian Rediscovers America
10. Adolf Shvedchikov: Parade of Life - poems in English and Russian
11. Adolf Shvedchikov: Overcoming Sorrow - poems in English and Russian
12. Sophia Dediu: Sophia meets Japan
13. Corneliu Leu: Roosevelt, Churchill, Stalin and Hitler: Their surprising role in Eastern Europe in 1944
14. Proceedings of the 5th International Conference "Computational Mechanics and Virtual Engineering" COMEC 2013
15. Georgeta Simion – Potanga: Beyond Imagination: A Thought-provoking novel inspired from mid-20th century events
16. Ana Dediu: The poetry of my life in Europe and The USA
17. Ana Dediu: The Four Graces
18. Proceedings of the 5th International Conference "Advanced Composite Materials Engineering" COMAT 2014
19. Sophia Dediu: Chocolate Cook Book: Is there such a thing as too much chocolate?

20. Sorin Vlase: Mechanical Identifiability in Automotive Engineering
21. Gabriel Dima: The Evolution of the Aerostructures – Concept and Technologies
22. Proceedings of the 6th International Conference "Computational Mechanics and Virtual Engineering" COMEC 2015
23. Sophia Dediu: Cook Book 1 A-B-C Common sense cooking
24. Sophia Dediu: Dim Sum Spring Festival
25. Ana Dediu and Sophia Dediu: Europe in 1985: A chronological and photographic documentary
26. Stefan Staretu: Europe: Serbian Despotate of Srem and the Romanian Area – Between the 14th and the 16th Centuries

New York: On W 34th St, Empire State Building (center back), Snoopy second on left, looking southeast.

www.ingramcontent.com/pod-product-compliance
Lightning Source LLC
Chambersburg PA
CBHW041358090426
42741CB00001B/12